READY TO EXPLORE KINGS CANYON?

APEX
L·E·G·E·N·D·S

ANNUAL 2020

THIS BOOK BELONGS TO:

ALFY

INDEPENDENT

ULTIMATE GUIDE

& UNOFFICIAL

APEX LEGENDS ANNUAL 2020
ISBN: 978-1-78106-714-7

Printed in Italy.

APEX LEGENDS

FAST FACTS

LET'S GET STARTED WITH A WHOLE BUNCH OF FACTS ABOUT THE WORLD'S FASTEST GROWING BATTLE ROYALE GAME...

Amazingly, Apex Legends was released into the world with no marketing, no big launch party and no advertising campaign! EA and Respawn Entertainment simply launched the game, and only then did the promotional onslaught begin!

The origins of Apex lie in a different game series altogether. Respawn Entertainment was previously responsible for the Titanfall videogames, and Apex Legends builds on ideas from those games. EA bought Respawn in 2017, and the plan for a Battle Royale-style game based around Titanfall came about at the same time.

YOU NEED TEAMWORK TO EMERGE VICTORIOUS IN APEX!

The game is set after the events of the game Titanfall 2. Titanfall 3 was postponed and possibly cancelled for good after the development of Apex.

7

It's estimated that EA made around $90m from Apex Legends within its first month of release. And that number has been growing ever since!

JUST ONE OF THE GAME'S LEGENDS

You might not think it, but every Legend – assuming they're not using a special skill – moves at exactly the same speed in the game!

The game was a very quick hit! Within a week, over 25 million people around the world had downloaded and played it. Within a month, that number had soared to a massive 50 million!

Apex Legends was first released on 4th February 2019 on PC, Xbox One and PlayStation 4. And as you more than likely know, it was launched as a free-to-play game from day one! Versions for the Nintendo Switch, iOS and Android were also discussed around the same time, but no further news on these versions has been released.

The first 'season' of Apex didn't actually start until over a month after the game was initially released. It launched on 19th March 2019 under the name Wild Frontier, and adopted the Battle Pass mechanic used by other Battle Royale titles, such as Fortnite.

The game has a number of playable Legends. However, one of them – Bloodhound – wasn't developed for Apex at all! He was originally intended for the first Titanfall game, as concept art of him came to light around that time. He had to wait until Apex before getting into a game proper, though!

Unlike its most obvious rival Fortnite, Apex Legends isn't going to be restricted to just one map. Within weeks of its launch, it was made clear that plans were afoot for other maps in the future. That said, the Kings Canyon map, with which the game launched, isn't short of places to visit!

As we'll discuss in more detail later, Apex differs in a couple of marked ways from its many rivals. For one, its ping system of communication is revelatory. Also, you can fall a great height and not take damage. No need for a glider here!

With one or two exceptions, you have to work hard to get decent weapons in Apex Legends. Guns are provided in their basic form, and it's up to you to acquire the mods and upgrades to give them extra punch. If you don't? Well, you're going to get outgunned pretty brutally by the end of the match!

DYING DOESN'T NECESSARILY MEAN DEATH

IT'S MORE OF A CLOSE COMBAT GAME THAN MOST BATTLE ROYALE TITLES

Each Battle Pass is set to come with around 100 rewards and will be unique to each season of the game. It's a cunning way to part you from your cash. Well, Apex Coins...

Apex demands teamwork! It has fewer players on the map than most Battle Royale games, and you must work in squads of three to succeed. You can still battle through if you go rogue and play by yourself, but it's a lot harder!

The game uses a variety of voice actors, some of which you may have heard before! Zehra Fazal, who voices the AI announcements in the game, has previously been heard on the likes of Uncharted 4 and Titanfall. J B Blanc (Caustic) turns up in Call Of Duty: Black Ops 4 and Mortal Kombat 11, whilst Lifeline's Mela Lee has popped up in Pillars Of Eternity II, Ghostbusters and more!

EA and Respawn are planning on supporting Apex Legends long term, in case you're worried about getting into a game and then it disappearing just as you become an expert at it! Look out for new seasons every three months or so, bringing with them new features, new cosmetic upgrades and occasionally new Legends too!

KNOW THE SCREEN

IT SOUNDS SIMPLE, BUT UNDERSTANDING WHAT THE SCREEN IS TELLING YOU DOESN'T HALF HELP IN A ROUND OF APEX! HERE'S WHAT YOU NEED TO KNOW...

1 You can easily call up the full version of the map, but this smaller view is always on screen and worth keeping an eye on. The yellow marker shows where someone has pinged a place to head for, and also note the position of the ring. You and your squadmates are marked as coloured arrows too.

2 The countdown to when the ring will next start closing in.

3 An indicator of where one of your teammates is. Note how our squad is close together, but still a little split. The arrow on the other side of the screen corresponds to our other squadmate.

4 Beneath the compass, note how there's a marker with a distance. We've previously pinged our target location, which is still a short distance away.

60   75   E   105   120   SE   150   165   S   195   210   SW

107
◇ 149M

4

5 SQUADS LEFT 👤 14

5

R RELOAD

⚡ 2m

8

GeMingZi

9

02
⌖ 100

G

1 TRIPLE TAKE   2   HAVOC

5 It's easy to lose track of this information – not just the number of squads remaining in the match, but the total number of active players too. As you can see, one squad appears to be a player down at the moment.

6 The shields and health of you and your teammates. If you notice they're struggling and you have spare resources, remember to share them out!

7 Shortcuts to your health and abilities, most notably...

8 ...that our Ultimate ability is charged and ready to go (we're playing as Gibraltar, who can call in an air assault).

9 The current state of your weapons. If one has an alternate fire mode, you'll get a signifier here.

101 THINGS TO DO IN APEX LEGENDS

CAN YOU TACKLE OUR LIST OF THINGS TO TRY IN APEX? CROSS EACH
ONE OFF AS YOU DO IT – AND SEE IF YOU CAN MANAGE ALL 101! HERE'S THE FIRST BATCH…

THERE'S A KILL FOR US RIGHT HERE, BUT CAN WE BECOME THE KILL LEADER?

1 Be the Jumpmaster! Don't surrender the chance at the onset of a match, and lead your team to a good starting position.

2 Land on a supply ship and get involved in the first big battle for loot. Bonus points if you survive it.

3 Or why not land in the ring right at the start of a match? Make sure you're armed and ready, though!

4 Just for once, separate from the rest of your squad for a jump. But don't go far – if they're landing in the middle of a location, perhaps start at the edge of it. Close enough to join forces, but far enough away that you're not fighting over the same loot.

5 Open up a supply bin and ping something for one of your squadmates.

6 Jump up a sharp ledge. It can sometimes take a bit of practice, but in Apex you can usually get a little higher than you might think possible.

7 Shoot someone whilst travelling along a zipline. Try not to get shot yourself!

8 Land a kill using one of the basic pistols – even more impressive if you haven't upgraded it at all!

9 Can you do damage to more than one enemy by throwing a grenade? Give it a go!

FEW THINGS ARE MORE SATISFYING THAN A GOOD MELEE ATTACK!

11 Slide your way down a very big hill for as long as possible without stopping.

12 Another climbing challenge! Run up a wall by springing at it, looking up and holding Jump. In Apex, climbing is a lot more straightforward than it may first appear.

10 Interrupt someone trying to land a finishing move on one of your team, then take them out!

13 Climb on top of an open door to reach a greater height.

14 Zipline to the top of a balloon, then jump off to rocket somewhere else on the map.

Note that you don't necessarily travel any further this way, just faster!

15 Play as Wraith and set up a dimensional rift for you and your teammates. It can take a while to get the hang of it.

16 Still playing as Wraith, set up a portal as a trap, place the exit at the end of a cliff, then try to lure an enemy through it.

17 Or become Caustic and fire off Nox gas to try to buy your team an advantage.

18 Use Pathfinder's survey beacon to let your team know where the ring is going to close in.

19 Play as Lifeline and call in a supply crate. For an added challenge, use it as an ambush – see if another squad is lured to it and take them out.

20 You don't need to, and often it's dangerous, but you should try a finisher move at least once. You do leave yourself open to attack, though.

21 Play as one of the locked characters. Remember you can grind your way to unlocking, rather than having to fork out cash!

22 Kill the Champion in a Battle Royale and bank the 500 XP that comes with it!

23 Become the Kill Leader – and that's a lot easier said than done!

24 Activate a knockdown shield when you're downed and find a way to safety.

25 Use an alternate fire mode, which you'll find on only a few weapons!

26 As tempting as it may be to make the game all about the weapons, down someone with a melee attack. It's surprisingly effective!

RECKON YOU CAN GET YOUR FACE ON THAT BANNER?

CONTINUED ON PAGE 30

MEET THE LEGENDS

APEX LEGENDS IS CONTINUALLY EVOLVING AND INTRODUCING NEW CHARACTERS, BUT HERE'S OUR GUIDE TO THE LEGENDS WHO GOT US ALL STARTED...

LIFELINE

Lifeline is the medic of the gang, so not someone you'd normally send onto the frontline into combat. That said, she's brilliant when someone takes a hit.

PASSIVE: Combat Media
When Lifeline revives one of the squad, she throws up a shield for extra protection, and applies medical kit 25% faster than any other Legend.

TACTICAL: Heal Drone
This can be sent to automatically heal teammates, although note that it will heal anyone in the area – friend or foe!

ULTIMATE: Care Package
She can call in a drop pod full of strong healing goodies. That said, any other player who spots it on the map can take advantage of it too!

ULTIMATE:
Dimensional Rift
Not the easiest skill to learn, but it lets you position two portals, then you and your squad can jump through. Ideal for a quick escape!

>>>>>>>>>>>>>>>>>>>>>>

WRAITH

Wraith is a bit of a utility player, and a first choice for a lot of players. She's good in attack, but also has the skills to get you out of a tight spot!

PASSIVE: Voices from the Void
One of our favourites, this alerts you when an enemy has marked your location, so you'll know they're coming!

TACTICAL: Into The Void
A skill that makes Wraith invisible (although her tracks are still viewable). Whilst you're in this void, you can't take damage, but it does take a small amount of time to activate, which leaves you vulnerable.

>>>>>>>>>>>>>>>>>>>>>>

ULTIMATE:
Ah, it's Rolling Thunder! A nice, big airstrike that hits a targeted area.

ULTIMATE:
Defensive Bombardment Gibraltar's airstrike is more precise than Bangalore's. It takes some time to call in, so isn't hard to avoid, but it does give the enemy something to worry about.

BANGALORE

An offensive character and just the kind of person you want leading you into battle!

PASSIVE: Double Time
This allows Bangalore to briefly run faster when she's taking hits. It's usually fast enough to get out of a firefight!

TACTICAL: Smoke Launcher
This explodes to give a cloud of very useful cover.

GIBRALTAR

The shielded fortress and primarily a defensive character, although one capable of holding his own in battle. Gibraltar isn't a bad choice for less experienced players, given that he can defend himself and isn't too bad in a scrap.

PASSIVE: Gun Shield
Activated when looking down the sights of a gun, this shield puts up a defence against incoming fire.

TACTICAL: Dome of Protection
Gibraltar can throw up a protective dome that lasts for 15 seconds, which is great when you're under attack or want a safe haven to do some healing.

BLOODHOUND

If you're less action inclined and more cunning, Bloodhound is the Legend for you. His abilities are all about hunting down and seeking out the enemy – and boy, is he good at it!

PASSIVE: Tracker
Bloodhound can uncover recent footprints and details such as when doors were opened, so you'll know when the enemy were last there. Handy!

TACTICAL: Eye of the Allfather
When Bloodhound deploys this, it will highlight any nearby enemies.

ULTIMATE:
Beast of the Hunt
With faster movement and super-sharp senses for tracking the enemy, it pays to listen when Bloodhound pings!

ULTIMATE:
Launch Pad
Arguably less useful than his tactical, Octane can deploy a launch pad to shoot any player into the air and get them out of a tight spot at speed. Use with care, though.

OCTANE

The first Legend to be added to the game after it initially launched, you have to unlock Octane. With the right ability, he's a speedy critter.

PASSIVE: Swift Mend
For every two seconds he goes without being hit, Octane recovers a point of health. Not bad, eh?

TACTICAL: Stim
For six very useful seconds, Octane can increase his speed by 30%. It comes at a price of 10 health points, but on the flip side it's keeping him alive!

ULTIMATE:
Vanishing Act
More decoys!
Lots more, in fact.
Mirage is cloaked,
then several
decoys appear.

Caustic must be unlocked too, and he's all about the gas, which makes him just the person to invite to a party, right?!

PASSIVE:
Nox Vision
When moving through a gas cloud, Caustic can still pick out the enemy, but this really needs to be used in conjunction with his tactical ability...

TACTICAL: Nox Gas Trap
Once placed, six Nox gas canisters will either go off when an enemy steps on them or you shoot at them. The gas causes slow damage.

MIRAGE

Another character you need to unlock, Mirage isn't the most popular of Legends, but he does have a useful trick or two up his sleeve.

PASSIVE: Encore!
When Mirage is knocked down, he's cloaked for five seconds and a decoy tries to remove the enemy from the scene.

TACTICAL: Psyche Out
This time, the decoy creates another Mirage, with the aim of distracting any foes who may be in the vicinity.

ULTIMATE:
Nox Gas Grenade
Packed full of
Nox gas, which will
spread over a large
area and damage
any enemies
caught in it.

ULTIMATE:
Zipline Gun
The ability to create a new zipline – extremely useful when the whole team needs to move fast!

>>>>>>>>>>>>>>>>>>>>>>

PATHFINDER

Effectively the satnav of the team, Pathfinder has some useful tricks to help the squad move around the map quickly.

PASSIVE: Insider Knowledge
Pathfinder scans the region to identify where the ring is next going to close in.

TACTICAL: Grappling Hook
This hook allows Pathfinder to move quickly in any direction or even pull enemies towards him.

>>>>>>>>>>>>>>>>>>>>>>

KNOW YOUR WEAP

IF YOU TRY TO BATTLE YOUR WAY THROUGH APEX WITH JUST A MOZAMBIQUE SHOTGUN, YOU'RE GOING TO RUN INTO TROUBLE! HERE'S OUR GUIDE TO WEAPONS...

HEAVY WEAPONS

WINGMAN
About the most effective pistol in the game, and brilliant if you're good at landing quick headshots. Each magazine holds six shots.

PROWLER BURST PDW
Features two firing modes – burst and automatic – but you should choose the auto mode. It's a sub machine gun with 20 shots per mag and a very fast firing rate.

ONS!

HEMLOK BURST AR

A popular weapon with both burst and single firing modes. It has a good firing rate, each mag holds 18 shots, and it can do fast damage to an opponent.

VK-47 FLATLINE

Not the easiest weapon to handle, but very effective in the right hands. It's an assault rifle that can hold 20 shots per magazine, with a super fast firing rate.

LONGBOW DMR

A sniper rifle that can do a lot of damage (110 if you land a headshot). It can hold five shots per mag, and for maximum effect couple it with the Skullpiercer Rifling hop-up.

M600 SPITFIRE

It's got a tricky recoil to manage, but the M600 is a strong light machine gun with a large magazine size of 35 and a good firing rate.

LIGHT WEAPONS

G7 SCOUT
A not uncommon sniper rifle, but with the weakest damage impact of them all. The standard magazine holds 10 shots, but there's no guarantee a headshot will do significant damage to an opponent.

R-99 SMG
No other mag has a rate of fire as high as the R-99. It's a sub machine gun, and a very popular one. What it lacks in damage, it makes up for in the number of shots it spits out in double-quick time!

P2020
A common weapon with a magazine size of 10. Its one advantage is that it doesn't have much recoil, making it easier to land a shot. It does so little damage, though, it's barely worth bothering!

RE-45 AUTO

An automatic pistol that's pretty decent early in the game, with a mag size of 15. It outlives its usefulness very early on, though.

ALTERNATOR SMG

It's got twin barrels and a recoil that allows less experienced players to manage firing. A mag size of 16 is pretty decent too.

R-301 CARBINE

It comes with dual fire modes, and the automatic option is the best. Each magazine holds 18, and it deals a rather potent headshot for a light weapon.

ENERGY WEAPONS

TRIPLE TAKE
With three bullets per shot, the Triple Take works as both a shotgun and a sniper rifle. It has a tight recoil and does reasonable damage.

HAVOC
A weapon that can hold two hop-ups, and each magazine for this solid rifle holds 25 shots.

DEVOTION
A light machine gun with a magazine of 44, you need to keep the trigger pulled to maximise its firing rate.

SHOTGUNS

EVA-8 AUTO
An automatic shotgun that sprays nine pellets in a single shot, with up to 10 damage points per pellet. It can be deadly in the right hands.

PEACEKEEPER
A shotgun with lots of power, 11 pellets per shot and a magazine that holds six shots. It's worth adding the precision choke hop-up for optimum effect.

MOZAMBIQUE
One of the weakest weapons in the game, this shotgun has low damage, a low fire rate and even its headshots don't do much. Better than nothing – just...

SPECIAL

There are two very rare Legendary weapons, and once you've used their ammo you can't get more! The Kraber .50-Cal sniper has a maximum headshot damage of an incredible 250. The Mastiff shotgun, meanwhile, holds four shots in its mag that each fire eight pellets to do up to 36 damage apiece with a single headshot!

PUZZLE PAGE

PIT YOURSELF AGAINST OUR TRICKY PUZZLES AND MAKE YOUR BRAIN LEGENDARY! **ALL OF THE ANSWERS ARE ON PAGE 92**

ANAGRAMS

CLARINET ESCORT
CLUE: APEX LEGENDS' PUBLISHER
_ _ _ _ _ _ _ _ _ _ _ _ _ _

THINK GREAT ACE
CLUE: AGGRESSIVE PING
_ _ _ _ _ _ _ _ _ _ _ _ _

ENTRAPMENT SEAT WINNER
CLUE: GAME CREATORS
_ _ _ _ _ _ _ _ _ _ _ _ _ _ _

RATLIKE PET
CLUE: THREE IS THE MAGIC NUMBER
_ _ _ _ _ _ _ _ _

EXAMS PAGE
CLUE: LEGENDS ARE MADE THERE
_ _ _ _ _ _ _ _ _

MR ENDED THOU
CLUE: A NOISY PLACE
_ _ _ _ _ _ _ _ _ _ _

DEAR ILL ELK
CLUE: THE DEADLIEST PLAYER IN THE GAME
_ _ _ _ _ _ _ _ _ _

BARTER GROUCH
CLUE: HOP-UP TO NO RECHARGE
_ _ _ _ _ _ _ _ _ _ _ _

CONGA SKINNY
CLUE: WHERE THE MAGIC HAPPENS
_ _ _ _ _ _ _ _ _ _ _

EXPAND GLEE
CLUE: WHAT WE ALL WANT TO BE
_ _ _ _ _ _ _ _ _

01

lmir20

damai

WORDSEARCH

CAN YOU FIND THESE LEGENDS & WEAPONS?

Bangalore	Gibraltar	Longbow	Pathfinder	Triple Take
Bloodhound	Havoc	Mastiff	Peacekeeper	Wraith
Caustic	Hemlok Burst	Mirage	Prowler Burst	
Devotion	Kraber	Mozambique	Scout	
Flatline	Lifeline	Octane	Spitfire	

101 THINGS TO DO IN APEX LEGENDS

PART 2

HOW LONG CAN YOU HIDE OUTSIDE THE RING FOR?

GET BACK IN THE RING!

27 Revive one of your teammates without taking a single hit.

28 Snipe an opponent and, even better, do it without them having a chance to shoot back.

29 Land a headshot! Can you do it from 500 metres away?

30 Land the first kill in a match.

31 Play as Caustic and win a match!

32 Can you win a match without using your character's Ultimate ability? Now THERE'S a challenge!

33 Set up a dome of protection when playing as Gibraltar, and get all of your squad under it and healing.

34 Use Mirage's vanishing act skill to turn a squad fight in your favour.

35 Make a kill with the Mozambique shotgun (which is regarded as pretty much the worst weapon in the game!).

36 Upgrade your gun with a hop-up attachment.

MIRAGE IS ABOUT – THERE'S A DECOY UP THERE

edoralia DECOY

39

Suggest a location for your squad to go to mid-match, and tick it off when they follow you there!

37 When the ring has closed in, hide on the outside of it for 30 seconds. Your health will take a hit, but it puts you in a decent strategic position to sneak up on someone!

38 Find a place on the map that's so high you go out of bounds and are told to return to the play area. Tip: go back to the play area quickly if you want to keep playing!

40 Drop three different items in a match to give to other players on your team.

41 Land some purple loot from a killed opponent's death box.

42 Find one of the small, hidden bots that are filled with loot, crack it open, then help yourself!

43 Use the precision choke on a shotgun to take out an opponent from distance!

44 Or just creep up behind an opponent and land a kill. Footsteps in Apex Legends are much quieter than in a game like Fortnite, so you stand a good chance of pulling this one off!

45 Learn to wiggle when standing still to make yourself harder to hit (it's easier on consoles, as you can slightly wiggle the analog stick).

46 Use the slide jump technique – arguably the fastest way to move around in Apex without using a special power – to escape a firefight!

47 Break an enemy's shield, then finish them off!

48 When you've been downed, use a ping to alert the rest of your squad to the exact location of your assailant.

49 Survive for 15 minutes in a match (which will earn you a solid pot of XP!).

50 Here's a tricky one: can you land the daily first kill bonus? This is awarded once for each character for the first kill landed every 24 hours. You're up against everyone else playing in the world, so it's tough!

51 Unlock and play as Octane.

CAN YOU LAND A LONG-RANGE HEADSHOT?

01:41

CONTINUED ON PAGE 44

WHERE TO FIND LOOT!

THE FIRST THING TO DO WHEN YOU LAND IS GET KITTED UP, WHICH MEANS THE HUNT IS ON FOR LOOT! BUT WHERE DO YOU FIND THE BEST STUFF? USING SEASON 1'S KINGS LANDING MAP AS A GUIDELINE, HERE'S WHERE TO LOOK...

DEATH BOXES ARE A GREAT SOURCE OF LOOT – AND ANY SHIELDS AND GUNS YOU PICK UP WILL BE FULLY PRIMED AND READY TO ROLL

HIGH VALUE, HIGH RISK

Without question, to get your paws on the best loot first, you're going to have to put yourself very much in the way of danger. At the start of a match, load up the map and look for two things. One is the area marked with a ring, the other is the supply ship flying across the map.

The supply ship – which appears again later in a game – is full of high-level loot. What's more – if you get your initial jump right – you can land right on top of it at the start of a match. Then, once you've bagged all the lovely loot, you can jump to the ground and start battling.

The ring also marks where some top-quality loot can be found at the start of a match. So if you land in the marked Hot Zone, you're likely to discover some very decent stuff. The problem with both of these locations? Well, let's just say they tend to be really rather popular! To put it bluntly, LOTS of squads have the same idea at the start of a match. As such, you're definitely

SUPPLY DROPS

As a match progresses, further supplies are dropped onto the battlefield. When you get an announcement that a supply drop is on its way, you quickly need to load up the map and look for a small blue circle. This will indicate where to head to get your hands on the fresh supplies.

Each drop will contain three items of loot, so there's a lot less to battle over than, say, the supply ship at the start of a match. But the upside to finding a supply drop is that you could get your mitts on some of the very best weapons in the game.

As always, be cautious: it's not just you who gets the notice of a supply drop landing, so there's a good chance another squad will be circling too. Still, it could be a game changer if you manage to get in there quick and nab yourself a nice Mastiff shotgun...

Skull Town
Mid Tier Loot

ONCE YOU OPEN IT, IT'S A SIGN TO ANYONE FOLLOWING THAT SOMEONE HAS ALREADY BEEN HERE

going to bump into someone else in both the Hot Zone and the supply ship.

There are two options here: one, arm up quickly and do battle. Two, hover around the outskirts, hope which ever team emerges from the rumble is sufficiently damaged, then try to take them out before they have a chance to recover – and steal all their lovely loot! It goes without saying that this is a very high-risk strategy, but if you manage to pull it off it's definitely the quickest way to get properly powered up early on in the game.

SUPPLY BINS

You'll come across supply boxes in most key locations. Sometimes you'll find a few together, so if you've managed to discover one, it might be worth having a quick scan to see if there's another nearby. These are common, but good for upgrades, health and ammunition. Beware if you find a supply box that's open, as it's a clear indication that somebody has been there before you, and chances are they're still lurking, especially at the start of a match.

HIGH LOOT LOCATIONS DO TEND TO ATTRACT OTHER SQUADS TOO

LOOT BOTS

You'll also find little robots dotted around the map, which contain a small amount of loot. These tend to be pretty hidden, but if you do manage to hunt one down, give them a whack or shoot them and they'll drop a few items. Generally, there's at least one decent piece of loot inside, so it's worth keeping your eyes and ears peeled at all times. Your ears in particular, as these little bots emit a distinctive sound, so you should know instantly when one is close by.

DROPPED STUFF

Take note after an opponent has been killed if the box of goodies they leave behind is glowing. This means it contains something better than you already have, and it glows the colour of the rarest item inside. It may still be worth looting even if it's not glowing – it just depends on whether you want to prioritise your search!

WE'RE IN EAST SETTLEMENT. NOT MUCH HERE, AS THE GAME DOESN'T EVEN ALERT US TO THE FACT THERE MAY BE DECENT LOOT ABOUT

East Settlement

PURPLE SUGGESTS THAT THE DEATH BOX HOLDS SOMETHING OF GREATER VALUE THAN WE ALREADY HAVE

Hold E Access Player Items

SEE? HALF-DECENT LOOT LIES AHEAD

The Cascades
Mid Tier Loot

THUNDERDOME GETS BUSY BECAUSE THERE'S USUALLY GOOD STUFF HERE

Thunderdome
ROUND 1
3:55

IF YOU DON'T NEED THE LOOT IN A SUPPLY BIN, PING IT!

AND FINALLY...

Appreciating that maps change between seasons, Apex will alert you when you enter a new part of the map if it's a high or medium loot area. You're pretty much guaranteed to find decent stuff if you head to a built-up area, particularly around the edges of the map. Thus, on the Kings Canyon map, Airbase, Artillery and Water Treatment all tend to be high loot areas.

Note that drops are randomised, but the probability of getting good stuff is still higher in some areas than others.

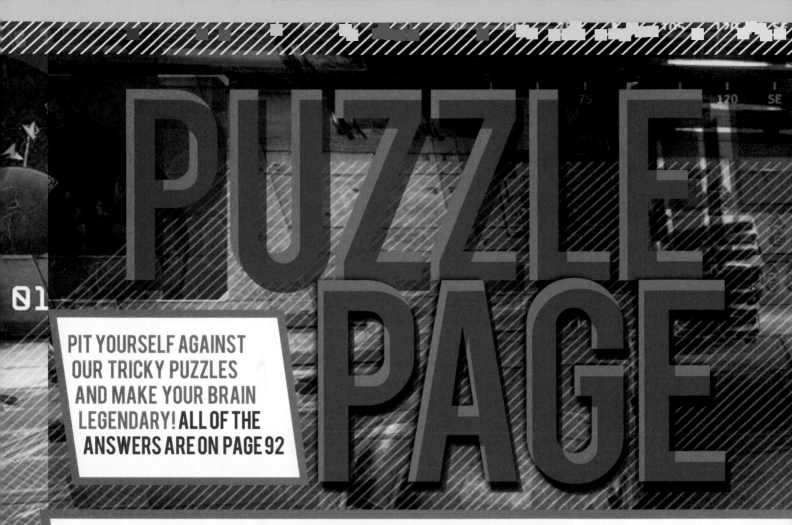

PUZZLE PAGE

PIT YOURSELF AGAINST OUR TRICKY PUZZLES AND MAKE YOUR BRAIN LEGENDARY! ALL OF THE ANSWERS ARE ON PAGE 92

THE POWER OF NINE – CAN YOU BECOME A PUZZLE LEGEND?

Can you complete these number grids, known as Sudoku? The aim of the game is to fill in the squares, with the numbers 1-9 appearing once in every one of the nine orange squares, and once on every line, both vertically and horizontally. Be legendary!

Grid 1

6	5	3	2	9				1
8	4	2		3				9
					4			
	1					3		
5		8			9		4	
	7					5		
		8						
7			5			1	3	6
			6	3	4	8	2	

Grid 2

		8		9				2
			6	5				
9			6	3	4			
4		9					7	
6		5		7	2	3		1
	3		6	9	5			8
			2	1	7			9
				5				3
7	9			4			1	8

Grid 1

1	4		5			7	9	3
2	3			8				
						1	8	
			1	7				4
	4	2	9	5	6			
9			6	4				
	7	2						
			6				5	
5	9	6			1		4	7

Grid 2

								3
7		4					2	8
	2	6	8		1		7	
	8				3			7
1			7	5	9			6
7		2					4	9
2	9		1		6	8	3	
6	5				7		9	
4								

Grid 3

	4	9	8		1			5
		1		4	6			8
		8	5		2	1		
8	7	6		5				
			8					
		7	4	9			2	
	4	9		8	5			
		4	1		2			
6		3		7	8	4	9	

Grid 4

3	6				4		8	
2		9		5				
	7						9	4
	9		4		2			
4		2	1		3	7		6
		5			7			2
	4							6
				2	1	8		4
	1		7				5	3

FANTASTIC
(AND ROUGHLY WHERE

WHEN PLAYING APEX, YOU NEED LOOT. LOTS OF LOOT. IT'S NOT ENOUGH TO HAVE A GOOD WEAPON, AS THEY ARRIVE IN PRETTY BASIC FORM. YOU HAVE TO UPGRADE THEM FOR A CHANCE OF SUCCESS. HERE'S OUR STARTER GUIDE...

AMMO

You'll find ammunition spread liberally around the map. Energy tends to be the rarest, whilst light and heavy ammo are in plentiful supply. If you're in a hurry, familiarise yourself with the colour-coding scheme! Brown is for light ammo, red is for shotgun shells, yellow is for energy ammo, and teal is for heavy ammo.

YOU'LL BE TOLD IF WHAT YOU FIND ISN'T AN IMPROVEMENT ON THE STUFF YOU ALREADY HAVE

13 SQUADS

You pinged loot: [

You pinged loot: [Heavy R

YOU HAVE A BETTER MAG   [FULL] HOLD X SWAP   PING

Attachment | Mag
EXTENDED HEAVY MAG
Slightly increases ammo capacity.

Weapons

LOOT
TO FIND IT!)

HOP-UPS

These attachments are generally specific to each weapon. Most guns don't have the option for one, but if they do they can greatly increase the damage they inflict.

PRECISION CHOKE: This tightens the spreads of bullets that come out of a gun, and works on both sniper rifles and shotguns.

SKULLPIERCER: If you're a dab hand at headshots, this one's for you. It increases headshot damage on compatible sniper rifles and pistols.

TURBOCHARGER: At the time of writing, this speeds up the fire rate of the notoriously sluggish Devotion and Havoc weapons.

ATTACHMENTS

BARREL STABILISERS: The recoil from different weapons varies, so it's worth finding a stabiliser to help with shot accuracy.

MAGAZINE ATTACHMENTS: The main advantage of a magazine attachment is to increase the number of bullets between reloads, but make sure you pick the right one for your gun. Shotgun Bolt is for shotguns, Extended Heavy Mag is for heavy weapons, and Extended Light Mag is for, well, you get the idea!

OPTIC ATTACHMENTS: These give you better aim when looking down the sights of your gun. Some work across every gun, others with specific weapons. A 3x optic will give you a mid-range shot, whilst specific sniper optics are for taking longer shots. Also look out for variable optics, which allow you to alter the amount of zoom.

STOCK ATTACHMENTS: These make your shots more accurate and improve the handling of your gun. Sniper Stock and Standard Stock are both available.

LOOK IN YOUR INVENTORY AND SEE WHAT EXTRAS YOU NEED

BACKPACKS

You'll need to find a backpack to give yourself some extra inventory slots. Without one, you'll end up having to stop mid-match to reorganise what you're carrying. Remember to ping if you find a bigger backpack and already have a smaller one!

SO YOU KNOW WHAT LOOT TO LOOK FOR, BUT WHERE DO YOU FIND IT? GLAD YOU ASKED...!

As we've mentioned elsewhere in this book, at the start of a match a few marked places are guaranteed to offer decent loot: the supply ship, Hot Zone and supply drops. But where else should you look for loot? Taking the Kings Canyon map from Season 1, we've dug out the best places to visit. The guiding ideas are the same: built-up places tend to offer the best returns, whilst smaller places on the outskirts will have something, but not much.

TOP TIP: READ THE SCREEN!
It sounds obvious perhaps, but you're notified when heading into an area with lots of loot, so it pays dividends to take note!

BEST PLACES
Aim for the big locations. The Airbase, for instance, has lots of outdoor areas, tonnes of supply bins and usually a fair few squads squabbling over it all too!

The Relay, meanwhile, is full of ziplines, so you need to keep your eyes peeled on the sky in case someone's flying overhead (which makes them a fairly easy target!). If you can reach the bit with the large satellite dish, you'll be rewarded with a pile of loot.

As for the Swamps, these are quite spread out, but they do have walkways in-between buildings. Again, a lot of it is out in the open, leaving you vulnerable to attack.

SUPPLY BINS AREN'T A BAD PLACE TO START—SOME ARE OUT IN THE OPEN, OTHERS NEED SEEKING OUT

WORTH EXPLORING

Thunderdome is a nice, quiet place to kit up. There's a decent amount of loot here, but generally not too many people looking for it.
The same goes for the Water Treatment plant, which has the downside of being far away from most other locations on the map (or an upside if you want to avoid bumping into other squads early in the game!).

DON'T GO OUT OF YOUR WAY

Places like the Shattered Forest are marked as areas of low-tier loot, and they're not kidding! On the one hand, this is a very off-peak part of the map, but your chances of finding much of use here are pretty remote. The same goes for the Market, which is at least a little more interesting as it's located indoors. It's a good location for an ambush, but you won't find the best stuff here! Well, unless you steal it from someone else...

THE HOT ZONE AND SUPPLY SHIP ARE THE BEST PLACES TO EXPLORE FOR LOOT AT THE START OF A MATCH

THIS IS A HIGHER LOOT AREA THAN YOU MAY THINK...

ARTILLERY
RELAY
SLUM LAKES
THE "PIT"
CASCADES
WETLANDS
RUNOFF
BUNKER
SWA
AIRBASE
BRIDGES
MARKET
HYDRO DAM
SKULL TOWN
REPULSOR
THUNDERDOME
WATER TREATMENT

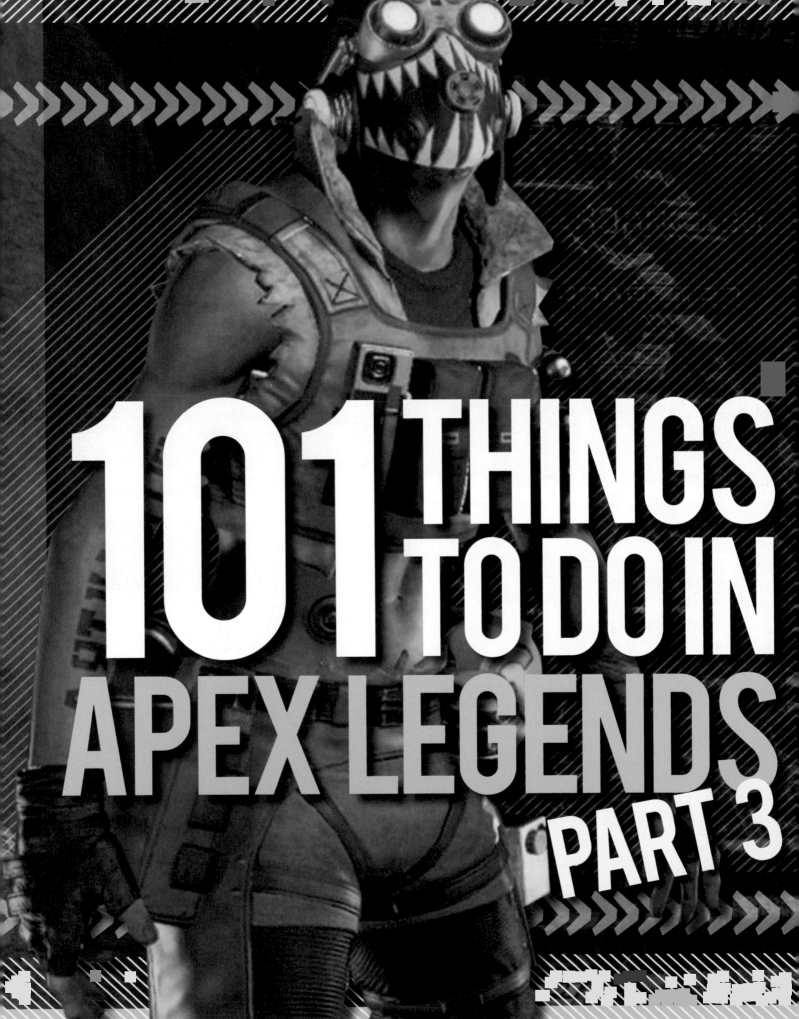

101 THINGS TO DO IN APEX LEGENDS PART 3

FANCY A NEW SKIN OR A COSMETIC CHANGE?

LEGENDS o   ARMORY   BATTLE PASS   STORE   0   4800   0

FEATURED   APEX PACKS   LEGENDS   APEX COINS

COSMETIC APEX PACK

Contains 3 items from the following categories:

- Weapon Skins
- Legend Skins
- Legend Finishers
- Banner Frames
- Banner Poses
- Banner Stat Trackers
- Intro Quips
- Kill Quips
- Crafting Metals

Probability of AT LEAST one:

- Rare or Better item: 100%
- Epic or Better item: 24.8%
- Legendary item: 7.4%

Additional Features:

- Guarantees at least one Legendary item drop for every 30 packs
- No Duplicate Cosmetics

PURCHASE
1 for 100

PURCHASE
10 for 1,000

APEX PACKS

ESC Back

57

Take time in the middle of a match to find a quiet(ish) spot and clean up your inventory – you might be grateful for this come the final skirmishes in the match!

52 Grind through 30 character levels (without buying a Battle Pass).

53 Visit a location on both sides of the map – in the same match!

54 Play a match where you let the game choose which Legend you are (simply by not making a choice yourself).

55 Call dibs on a piece of loot after another player has alerted you to it.

56 Go through a match without taking a single item from a supply bin.

58 Take on and win a fight with an opponent when you have no armour!

59 Change the skin of your favourite Legend.

60 And while you're there, change the skin of your favourite weapon in the game too!

UH-OH—HERE COMES A FINISHING MOVE

61 Find and equip a piece of gold equipment.

62 Ping an empty slot in your inventory to alert your team that you're after something!

63 Alert your squad to at least 20 useful items in one match (although the game doesn't tally the score for you, so you'll have to do that).

64 Find and use a Phoenix Kit to fully revive your Legend.

65 Find an Ultimate Accelerant, then give it to Lifeline!

66 Understand the damage colour-coding system, then zero in on an opponent with no shields.

67 Spot the enemy before the rest of your team, then ping their location to your squad.

68 Kill more opponents than anyone else in your team.

69 Survive to the last three squads, even when someone has quit the match and left you with two players (grrrr!).

70 Discover the ten Nessy plushies hidden around the Kings Canyon map. And on that...

71 ...shoot those Nessies in the right order to unlock a very special Easter Egg in the game!

72 Earn 1000 Legend tokens.

73 Bring a teammate back to life by taking their banner to a beacon.

74 Save two of your team in the same match, then count up the bonus XP!

75 Block a door with a downed teammate to delay the opposition getting inside!

76 Interrupt someone performing a finishing move...

SOMEONE MIGHT NEED TO BE RESPAWNED HERE

CONTINUED ON PAGE 62

ESSENTIAL BATTLE TIPS

WHEN YOU HEAD TO THE BATTLEFIELD, YOU'LL NEED AS MUCH INTEL AND KNOWHOW AS YOU CAN MUSTER, SO HERE ARE OUR TOP TIPS TO SUCCESSFUL COMBAT...

HERE WE'VE GOT A SPLIT SQUAD THAT'S NOT QUITE WORKING TOGETHER AT THE MOMENT...

STAY CLOSE, BUT...

As we've said before, this is a squad-driven Battle Royale game, so a team that plays together is going to stand a better chance of success. If you work together, share goodies, and keep an eye on each other's shields and health, it's possible to win a Battle Royale by killing just three or four opponents between you. Gibraltar's protective dome or Lifeline's healing bot are both potential lifesavers, so it's worth having at least one of these in your squad, possibly even both!

But remember, you DON'T want to stand side by side, where one projectile weapon can take out the lot of you in one hit. Spread yourselves out. Inevitably, as squads come in odd numbers, someone will be isolated, so try to keep the entire team within the space of the mini-map at the top left of the screen.

STAY TOGETHER DURING
THE INITIAL JUMP

TALKING TACTICS

As good as the pinging system is (and it really is!), it's no substitute for people talking to each other in real time. A huge word of warning here, though. Avoid using a headset and having a conversation with someone you don't know. Instead, team up with people you do know if you intend to use voice chat. It allows you to be more precise with instructions, chatter and ideas, although the ping system is a very good second place solution!

WATCH WHO EVERYONE CHOOSES
IF YOU'RE PICKING LAST

SELECT LEGEND

2

YOU ARE P

3R

BALANCE YOUR SQUAD

We can't say this enough: the ideal squad will have one Legend devoted to healing or shielding, and one offensive character who can handle themselves in a fight. Appreciating that new Legends are set to come on board in the coming months, do bear this in mind. If you're choosing last, as well as instantly becoming the Jumpmaster, you need to pay attention to the two characters already picked before zeroing in on yours.

RUN INTO FIGHTS

This might sound like a daft piece of advice, but there is an advantage to getting involved in an ongoing scrap between two squads. Apex Legends doesn't reward overly defensive tactics, and once you're armed up, running towards a battle is likely to interrupt opponents who have already taken damage. Furthermore, if the battle is ongoing, they might not have had much chance to heal up, nor, if you're lucky, will they have a lot of ammunition left. The key is to take opponents at their weakest, and running into a fight – whilst fraught with risk – is a good way to do so.

WE HAVE TWO ATTACKING CHARACTERS AND ONE DEFENSIVE ONE IN OUR SQUAD

BANGALORE
PROFESSIONAL SOLDIER

BLOODHOUND GIBRALTAR LIFELINE PATHFINDER OCTANE

WRAITH BANGALORE CAUSTIC MIRAGE

GIBRALTAR   NOW SELECTING

JUMPING

If you're the Jumpmaster, aim for a target that your squad actually has a chance of reaching. There's no point starting a battle if you're stuck in the middle of nowhere and totally exposed. Aim for an area on the map that's a maximum of 1000 metres away. Any further, and be prepared to fall short.

TARGET AN INDIVIDUAL ENEMY

Remember, if possible, the squad should isolate one opponent rather than focusing on taking out an entire squad. Empty your magazines into the individual and take them out of the game, which will instantly weaken the rival team. If you spread out the battles, you're reliant solely on individual performances rather than team play.

PLAY EACH PLAYER TO THEIR STRENGTHS

14 SQUADS LEFT 36

THE FINAL BATTLE

When you're down to the last two or three squads, it pays to be a little more cautious. If you go all cavalier now, you're likely to be picked off quite easily, so hold back. Get your squad repaired and ready for battle. If you can position yourself behind a door, and let the other side attack you, it could work in your favour. But you need to stay close and focused, and pick off the enemy carefully. Don't rule out projectiles at this stage, as they may just put the opposition on the back foot.

DON'T QUIT!

We've played matches where our squad was seemingly on its last legs, with little chance of success, where two players needed respawning at once, and defeat was staring us in the face. And you know what? That was a match we won! Remember, never give up! Don't quit until your squad has been eliminated and there's no way back, because with Apex Legends you never quite know what can happen...!

MARK ENEMIES SO YOUR SQUADMATES KNOW WHERE THEY ARE TOO

I f there's one huge feature Apex Legends has brought to the world of Battle Royale games, it's the amazing ping system for communicating with your teammates.

Rather than having to rely on people wearing a headset with voice chat enabled, squads can now work together without having to actually talk to one another. It's much safer, as you never quite know who you might be talking to.

THE BASICS

If you're struggling to get to grips with pinging, head over to the game's tutorial again and have a play with the system there. You need to use the middle mouse button if you're playing on PC, or the R1 or right shoulder button on consoles.

At its simplest, the system lets you mark a spot on the map and ping it. Your teammates are then alerted to an area to explore. If you ping whilst your crosshairs are on an item of loot, your team will be told what that item is (useful if it's high tier loot!). Likewise, if your crosshairs are over an enemy and you ping, it gives your squad the location of the foe.

THAT'S JUST THE KIND OF LOOT WORTH PINGING, ALTHOUGH IN THIS CASE WE NEED IT OURSELVES

PING PING PING!

GET TO KNOW THE PING SYSTEM AND ITS ADVANCED FEATURES!

DIBS!

When a teammate pings that they've found an item, you'll be told what it is and where to find it. If you ping on the ping, you can call dibs on it. It's not going to stop another teammate running in and grabbing it, it just lets everyone know that it's an item you're interested in.

NOTE SOMEONE HAS PINGED A LOCATION 46 METRES AWAY. BEST HEAD THERE...

ANYONE NEED A SPARE HELMET?

ADVANCED PINGING

If you double-tap on the ping button, you can place a more specific marker on the map to give your squadmates a little more information. These can mark the general area an enemy is in, indicate where you're looting, note that somebody has been in the spot you're in, or just say you're watching over an area.

What's more, if you open up your inventory, you can ping to request items in case a squadmate has any spare. So if you need an attachment for your weapon, hover over the space for it on your inventory screen and press ping.

It's fiddly at first, but definitely worth getting to know, especially in the end-game, when your squad needs to be at its very best!

PUZZLE PAGE

PIT YOURSELF AGAINST OUR TRICKY PUZZLES AND MAKE YOUR BRAIN LEGENDARY! **ALL OF THE ANSWERS ARE ON PAGE 92**

01

ANAGRAMS

DIVE ONTO
CLUE: POWERFUL WEAPON
_ _ _ _ _ _ _ _ _

RAMJET SUMP
CLUE: YOU DECIDE
_ _ _ _ _ _ _ _ _ _

AD ACCESS
CLUE: WATERY LOCATION
_ _ _ _ _ _ _ _

EYEBALL TAROT
CLUE: GAME TYPE
_ _ _ _ _ _ _ _ _ _ _

HYDRA MOD
CLUE: GENERATING POWER
_ _ _ _ _ _ _ _

RIP DAFT HEN
CLUE: MRVN
_ _ _ _ _ _ _ _ _

BEAST SPLAT
CLUE: GET WHAT YOU NEED
_ _ _ _ _ _ _ _ _

CLONKED KID SHOWN
CLUE: PROTECTION
_ _ _ _ _ _ _ _ _ _ _ _

NU BOLD HOOD
CLUE: MYSTERIOUS HUNTER
_ _ _ _ _ _ _ _ _

FIERCER KILL SLURPING
CLUE: BETTER HEADSHOTS
_ _ _ _ _ _ _ _ _ _ _ _ _ _

54

WORDSEARCH

CAN YOU FIND THESE APEX LEGENDS LOCATIONS?

Airbase	Relay	Swamps
Artillery	Repulsor	The Pit
Bridges	Runoff	Thunderdome
Cascades	Skull Town	Water Treatment
Hydro Dam	Slum Lakes	Wetlands

V	L	I	O	R	N	S	I	K	T	T	H	U	N	D	E	R	D	O	M	E
R	I	T	A	X	F	E	W	N	L	R	Y	W	H	R	P	M	Y	X	X	S
Z	S	W	S	M	N	A	P	D	V	V	D	S	K	A	B	W	O	H	B	A
M	O	P	A	W	L	J	I	K	A	C	R	E	D	V	V	N	F	D	R	B
M	Y	S	A	T	I	P	E	H	T	U	O	A	X	N	R	D	H	T	T	R
G	N	Y	M	G	E	U	D	M	E	D	D	Z	Q	O	A	Q	I	B	Z	I
L	T	K	R	W	N	R	T	J	I	K	A	Z	Z	R	T	L	W	L	G	A
O	G	S	T	D	D	J	T	T	V	C	M	S	R	L	L	L	R	T	F	Y
R	K	E	P	W	H	T	A	R	Y	O	H	A	F	E	U	I	S	E	G	G
W	Q	G	M	I	I	K	P	U	E	S	G	U	R	X	G	H	N	X	W	U
Z	W	D	L	X	X	E	N	N	G	A	A	Y	S	R	A	W	F	H	V	A
I	N	I	B	G	C	J	N	O	H	H	T	U	D	T	N	F	G	O	V	M
V	Y	R	W	N	D	M	M	F	O	Z	U	M	B	F	G	G	R	N	Q	E
X	E	B	L	K	H	U	S	N	F	O	O	Z	T	E	E	U	L	W	J	K
E	S	E	I	F	Q	J	S	O	U	L	B	Z	X	N	O	O	U	S	F	L
L	S	O	T	U	A	V	L	L	R	C	D	Y	Z	R	T	O	W	P	V	T
O	S	P	M	A	W	S	M	A	Y	S	P	A	M	L	U	O	E	Q	W	D
V	K	L	B	B	N	Y	R	J	E	S	L	G	L	S	K	K	G	C	K	M
S	O	J	G	F	V	O	V	G	R	W	T	U	Z	C	E	I	I	A	G	D
W	K	I	K	A	S	H	G	D	A	M	K	Y	M	D	A	V	G	S	T	T
J	Q	X	Q	L	Z	Q	B	Y	V	S	V	E	D	L	O	Q	D	C	B	X
J	X	H	U	L	Z	U	F	A	J	Y	C	Q	N	A	A	S	L	A	F	V
B	I	P	X	C	M	U	V	L	I	I	E	M	O	J	N	K	P	D	P	P
U	E	W	S	M	J	W	T	E	W	O	S	D	Z	Z	W	I	E	E	H	H
R	L	O	O	Y	W	O	Z	R	R	R	X	R	S	N	K	I	B	A	S	D	W

WHEN YOU'RE HIT!

YOU'RE NOT GOING TO WIN EVERY SKIRMISH, BUT EVEN WHEN YOU'RE DOWN YOU'RE NOT NECESSARILY OUT!

WE'RE UNDER ATTACK, AND AS THE ARROW SHOWS WE'RE BEING HIT FROM THE LEFT. WHEN KNOCKED DOWN, REMEMBER YOU CAN STILL PING AN ENEMY'S LOCATION

KNOCKED DOWN
166 DAMAGE INFLICTED

BLEEDING OUT

T he intensity of battles in Apex means you'll inevitably end up taking damage, and you may even be knocked down or killed. But there are still a few things you can do should the worst happen...

PATCH YOURSELF UP

The first thing to do if you take a bit of damage is repair it. Any shields will be depleted first and, if you don't have any, your overall health will be in danger of falling to zero.

Obviously, you need to find a way to repair both, but make sure you're away from enemies when you do. It can take a short while to patch yourself up, so sitting out in the open is asking for trouble. Hide yourself away or get Gibraltar to throw up a protective shield and repair yourself inside.

The best way to repair yourself is with a Phoenix Kit. This takes time to apply, but brings both your shields and health up to the maximum of 100. Alternatively, a medkit fully restores your health, and a shield battery has the same effect on your shields. And don't overlook syringes and shield cells, which are great for quick repairs when it's not safe to wait around too long.

KNOCKDOWN SHIELD

If you've been shot and are in need of recovery, deploy a knockdown shield if you have one. This stops enemies inflicting further damage on you, providing you aim the shield in their direction. You still need recovery from a teammate, and if you don't move fast another player can nip around the side of the shield and take you out completely. But it gives you some defence in the midst of a firefight and keeps you alive – when used properly – that little bit longer.

LIFELINE

If you have Lifeline in your squad, you'll have access to even more revival options. She's the combat medic of the group, and as well as having a healing drone at her disposal, she can call in a care package as her Ultimate ability. This drops medical supplies from the sky, although other squads may notice it too!

If Lifeline's in your line-up, she should be your number one choice for reviving downed comrades. Her Passive ability sees her throw up a protective shield when she's reviving someone, which is very handy when other squads and players are about.

RECOVERY

If you've been knocked down and are bleeding out, your teammates have a short amount of time to revive you. You're still able to ping when down and let the squad know the enemy's location. However, the worst thing they can do is rush straight in to revive you, as the person who downed you is still likely to be in the area, hungry for another kill. They may need to clear the area first before saving you. Yes, you could 'die' in that time but, of course, in Apex that isn't the end…!

OUR SHIELDS ARE DOWN AND WE'RE TAKING DAMAGE FROM AHEAD

STAYING ALIVE!

Don't forget, you need to share your loot! This is particularly important when it comes to shields and health. Make sure you ping if you find healing items. Don't assume everyone else, even late in the game, is fully stocked. It's better to be alerted to an item you don't necessarily need than to be caught short when you need it the most.

FIND A SAFE SPACE TO HEAL – THIS IS A LITTLE MORE OUT IN THE OPEN THAN WE'D LIKE

REVIVAL

In Apex, death doesn't have to mean death! If you bleed out on the battlefield, another member of your squad can pick up your banner and take it to a respawn point on the map. They have a finite amount of time to collect your banner, so keep an eye on the countdown that starts to tick. As always, approach respawn points with caution, as they're very much out in the open. Enemy squads have been known to camp around them too or target a sniper rifle in their direction.

IF ALL ELSE FAILS, HOLSTER YOUR WEAPONS AND RUN. MIGHT NOT DO US MUCH GOOD HERE, THOUGH

HOW DO I SURVIVE

ROUND 2 - CLOSING 2.20

CARE PACKAGES ATTRACT ATTENTION, BUT ALWAYS CONTAIN SOMETHING USEFUL

Matches in Apex Legends can feel a little different to those in other Battle Royale games. For starters, the map has fewer players on its core form, so unless you head straight to high loot areas, there's a good chance you won't encounter another squad for some time.

So if you're looking for some quick tips on making it to the end-game and giving yourself a decent crack at winning, read on...

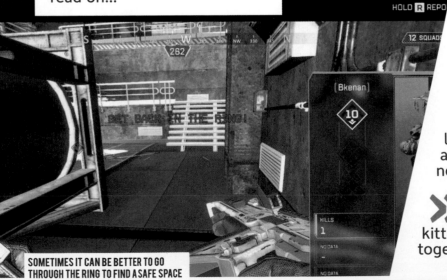
SOMETIMES IT CAN BE BETTER TO GO THROUGH THE RING TO FIND A SAFE SPACE

>> Don't go looking for trouble early in the match. Head to a location on the edge of the map, then work your way in, bearing in mind that the ring will begin closing in. When jumping onto the map at the start of a match, remember to look around you. If other squads look to be landing in your chosen location, don't be afraid to change your plans and head where no-one else is landing.

>> It's obvious, but worth saying again and again: spend the early part of a battle kitting up, share the loot between you, work together, and communicate!

THE TACTICS THAT HELP YOU WIN OTHER BATTLE ROYALE GAMES MAY NOT LEAD TO VICTORY IN APEX, SO HERE ARE A FEW SURVIVAL TIPS AND TRICKS...

LONGER?

'RE RESPAWNED, NOTE ENO WEAPONS!

PICK YOUR FIGHTS. ER, NOT LIKE THIS ONE...

>> When you spot an enemy, don't fire straightaway, unless they've seen you, of course. Instead, ping their location to your squad, so the whole gang's ready for the upcoming gunfight. But don't be afraid to walk away from a battle if you think your team can't win it.

>> Remember that it can sometimes be worth running towards a firefight should you hear gunfire in the distance. But take your time, and don't run straight into the midst of a battle. It will usually be two squads doing damage to each other, and the best time to attack is when only one of those teams is left standing. Chances are they'll have taken a lot of hits, so you just need to go in and blast them before they get a chance to heal up! It's a good way to stack the odds in your favour.

>> As we've said before, you WILL have to head into battle sooner or later. You can survive a long time skulking around the edges and hiding, but you're not going to win any match that way. Just remember to pick your fights, choose the right moment and work together. Can you ambush another team? Can you force them into a tight space and lie in wait? Try to fight all ultimate battles on your terms and in your favour. And good luck out there, Legends!

A GOOD PLACE FOR
AN AMBUSH...

101
TO DO IN
APEX LEGENDS
PART 4

PEOPLE CAN SEE YOU COMING WHEN YOU USE A BALLOON...

77 Interrupt an opponent performing a finishing move by lobbing a grenade at the perfect moment.

78 If you're playing as Pathfinder, use his grappling hook to pull an opponent towards you at speed!

79 Set up a zipline as Pathfinder to get the entire team out of a tight spot.

80 Aim a zipline to attach to another zipline. Now THAT'S a tricky shot to get right!

81 Aim at a destination 1000 metres away when you first jump off, and manage to get all the way there!

82 Heal yourself whilst in the midst of a long slide. It's possible to do!

83 Find a small building and hide inside, setting an ambush for an enemy team!

84 Kill an enemy as soon as they're downed – before they get a chance to recover.

85 Or wait and see if someone tries to revive them, then take BOTH of them out! Reckon you can do that?

WATCH FOR THE GRAPPLING HOOK...

RECOVER 4

89
Take no damage at all in a single match, and make it to the last three squads.

86
When you're landing from a great height, hit the melee button just as you touch down to speed up your landing!

87
Take out an opponent just as they land from jumping off a balloon. They leave a trail behind them, so you'll know they're coming!

88
Have two guns on the go that use two different types of ammunition (which is a good practical tip anyway!).

90
Get the extra experience bonus by putting together a squad of three people who all know each other.

91
Discover and use a Phoenix Pack to refuel your shields and health in one go!

92
Share a health pack or key inventory item with another member of your squad.

93
Inflict over 300 damage in one match.

94 Emerge triumphant in a match where you've had to be respawned.

95 Tricky one, this. Can you get to the end of a match with not just three kills, but at least two revives or respawns to your name as well?

96 Open eight supply bins in a single match.

97 Stay still for 20 seconds and take out an opponent. You'll need some really good cover to pull this off, though!

98 Here's a tough, tough challenge: win a match of Apex Legends without sending a single ping. Yikes!

99 Land a kill with a Kraber-1, although make your shot count, as the reload time on it is lengthy!

100 That, or take someone out with the game's other original Legendary weapon, the mighty Mastiff shotgun.

101 And you can guess this one: win a match and emerge with your squad as Champions! Good luck, Legends...

WELL DONE, CHAMP!

YOU ARE THE
CHAMPION

There are four tiers of skins for Legends and weapons, at varying prices and levels of exclusivity, and you can get you hands on them in three different ways:

» **Using the crafting metals you get in Apex Packs**
» **Using Apex Coins, which are bought with real money and can be used in the Rotating Shop**
» **Using Legend Tokens, which are earned through playing**

Skins that look pretty similar to the default designs fall into the Common tier and cost just 30 crafting metals. Rare tier skins offer a little more customisation, such as the different fabrics in Bloodhound's Tartan Fleece skin, and cost 60 crafting metals. Epic tier skins cost 400 crafting metals, and Legendary tier skins, which are the most modified and rarest, cost 1200 crafting metals or 1800 Legend Tokens.

» **Octane** has two racing-inspired skins called Gold Rush and The Victory Lap – the former in black, sky blue, gold and grey, and the latter in bright blue, white, yellow, orange and black. Both give him a robot-esque look. His other Legendary skins are Speed Demon and El Diablo.
» **Mirage** has the bright yellow body suit of The Revenger and the metallic anime-inspired body suit of Ghost Machine, whilst a more out-of-doors form of the Legendary skin can be found in the red and black of The Prestige or the green, brown and blacks of Angel City Hustler.
» **Bloodhound**'s Legendary skins are an imaginative mash of plague doctors, Chinese/Japanese imperial armour and the gothic, such as The Imperial Warrior, Royale Guard, The Plague Doctor and The Runekeeper.
» **Caustic** has some interesting skins that play with textures and fabric, such

SKINS!

IF YOU'RE LOOKING TO SHOW OFF YOUR FAVOURITE LEGEND OR WEAPON ON THE BATTLEFIELD, YOU'LL NEED TO KNOW HOW TO GET THE BEST SKINS IN APEX!

ADS LEFT 👤 ?

OCTANE SPEED DEMON

BLOODHOUND THE PLAGUE DOCTOR

GIBRALTAR DARK SIDE

WRAITH VENGEANCE SEEKER

LIFELINE REVOLUTIONARY

5 GREAT LEGENDS SKINS!

as the black furry outfit and gold gas mask of Blackheart, the garish blue fur of Philosopher's Stone, and the crisp silky gold and white of Divine Right and Sixth Sense.

» **Gibraltar**'s skins range from the generic Millennium Tusk to those that convey his Maori background and backstory, such as Bunker Buster, Ride or Die and perhaps the best skin so far: Dark Side.

» **Pathfinder** has two models of skin: the squarer and rugged brown Model P or the blue The Aviator, as well as the smoother humanoid skins of the metallic Quicksilver and red race car-inspired Angel City Pacer.

» **Bangalore** has uniform skins inspired by her character's history, such as The Enforcer and Officer Williams, alongside heavier outfits, like Apex Overdrive and The Spacewalker.

Lifeline has a variety of fashionable Legendary skins, such as London Calling, Organized Anarchy, Vital Signs and Peak Performer, which are all imaginative without changing her character.

» **Wraith** has the pink and metallic Void Specialist or white and red Quarantine 772, both of which are similar to her default outfit, but a better investment would be the shaved head and combat-ready Vengeance Seeker or The Liberator.

LEDREZ ALTERNATOR

LEGENDARY HAVOC SKIN
SILVER STORM

HAVOC THE SILVER STORM

PEACEKEEPER THE LONESTAR

5 GREAT WEAPON SKINS!

WEAPONS

The variety of Legendary weapon skins is vast when it comes to assault rifles – look out for the Hemlok's Lost Queen, the R-301's The Daybreaker and both steampunk Havoc skins. The most appealing skins for submachine guns are the Alternator's LED Rez, the R-99's The Alchemist, and the incredible Egyptian-inspired The Dark Realm and The Lightworker for the Prowler. The best for light machine guns is the Devotion's Nitro Kustom, and the highlights for sniper rifles are both the G7 Scout's The Golden Dragon and Cold Justice, plus the Triple Take's First Strike. Some of the best shotgun skins are the EVA-8 Auto's The Bone Collector and the reptile-like Guardian of Atlantis. Legendary pistol skins include the P2020's Romeo & Juliet-inspired Lady Justice and the lion design of the RE-45's The Pride.

Not surprisingly, some of the best weapons have the best skins. The Mastiff's Warp Zone, the Peacekeeper's The Lonestar and the Spitfire's RAF-inspired Flying Warhawk are all beautiful cosmetics.

M600 SPITFIRE FLYING WARHAWK

PROWLER THE DARK REALM

REWARDS

So what can you get besides the usual tiers of skins? Well, just look at the goodies that came with Season 1 of the Battle Pass, Wild Frontier. Whilst every player got the Messenger Octane skin at Level 48, those who paid for the Battle Pass (950 Apex Coins) or Battle Pass Bundle (2800 Apex Coins) got three exclusive skins – Lifeline's Revolutionary skin, Mirage's Outlaw skin and Wraith's Survivor skin – which were removed when the season ended in June 2019.

Beyond these, there are over 20 weapon skins to be gained for passing each level. In Season 1, Level 2, it was the Triple Take's Harvest, at Level 9 it was the Prowler's Navigator, at Level 44 it was the Alternator's Patchwork, at Level 51 it was the Prowler's Thrill of the Hunt, and at Levels 100 and 110 there were two new special skins: the Havoc's Silver Storm and Golden Idol. Different weapon effects can even be unlocked by one kill, three kills, then five kills – perhaps the most unique reward offered by Respawn so far!

PUZZLE PAGE

PIT YOURSELF AGAINST OUR TRICKY PUZZLES AND MAKE YOUR BRAIN LEGENDARY! **ALL OF THE ANSWERS ARE ON PAGE 92**

One thing that's essential in Apex Legends is visual acuity – the ability to see and interpret things quickly. So why not pit yourself against these six puzzles by identifying which of the options on the right corresponds to the picture on the left? Good luck!

WHO CAN GIVE YOU A DOME OF PROTECTION?

THE BIG APEX LEGENDS: QUIZ

HOW WELL DO YOU KNOW APEX? HAVE A GO AT OUR QUIZ TO FIND OUT WHETHER YOU'LL BE DOWNED IN THE FIRST MINUTE OR SUCCEED AS A BATTLE ROYALE CHAMPION!

1

On the mechanics of which earlier gaming series is Apex Legends based?

A Titanfall
B Battlefield
C FIFA

2

What's the name of the development company behind Apex?

A Epic Games
B Rare
C Respawn Entertainment

5 Which of these Legends wasn't in the first release of the game?

A Octane
B Bloodhound
C Wraith

6 In what year was Apex first released?

A 2017
B 2018
C 2019

THIS ISN'T A LEGENDARY WEAPON, BUT DO YOU KNOW WHAT IS?

4 What was Season 1 called?

A Wild Frontier
B Wild West
C Wild Battle

3 What's the name of the game's first map?

A Kings Landing
B Kings Canyon
C Kings Causeway

7 What's the communication system called?

A Pong
B Ping
C Pang

8
How many players take part in a traditional Apex Battle Royale match?

A 60
B 72
C 100

14
Which of these is a Legendary weapon?

A VK-47 Flatline
B Kraber
.50-cal sniper
C Wingman

HOW MANY PLAYERS TAKE PART IN ONE MATCH?

9
Which of these Legends can fire a zipline?

A Caustic
B Pathfinder
C Gibraltar

10
Whose Ultimate ability is Rolling Thunder?

A Bangalore
B Gibraltar
C Lifeline

13
Which Legend can throw up a Dome of Protection?

A Gibraltar
B Lifeline
C Bloodhound

11
Which of these tops up both your shields and health to 100?

A Phoenix Kit
B Syringe
C Care Package

WHAT DO YOU NEED TO RESPAWN A PLAYER?

12
Which Legend can see through Nox gas?

A Wraith
B Octane
C Caustic

THE BIG APEX LEGENDS QUIZ!

15

The Arc Star explodes after how many seconds?

A One
B Two
C Three

20

Which item can give you protection once you're downed?

A Knockdown shield
B Syringe
C Phoenix Kit

16

Which of these currencies can't you use in Apex Legends?

A Legend Tokens
B V-Bucks
C Apex Coins

17

What's the name of the achievement for winning a match with each of the different Legends?

A Apex Emperor
B Apex Champion
C Apex Legend

19

Who leads your squad in the initial drop to the map?

A Pathfinder
B Jumpmaster
C Explorer

18

What needs taking to a respawn point to bring a character back to life?

A Heart
B Flag
C Banner

HOW DID YOU DO?

1	A
2	C
3	B
4	A
5	A
6	C
7	B
8	A
9	B
10	A
11	C
12	A
13	A
14	B
15	C
16	B
17	C
18	C
19	B
20	A

Score:

18-20 You truly are a Legend!

12-17 You made the final few squads, but still have a little way to go.

8-11 A solid performance, but a few upgrades and hop-ups wouldn't hurt.

3-7 Back to the training ground for you, friend!

0-2 Your battle ended quickly. More practice required!

ANSWER PAGES

CLARINET ESCORT
ELECTRONIC ARTS

ENTRAPMENT SEAT WINNER
RESPAWN ENTERTAINMENT

EXAMS PAGE
APEX GAMES

DEAR ILL ELK
KILL LEADER

CONGA SKINNY
KINGS CANYON

THINK GREAT ACE
ATTACKING HERE

RATLIKE PET
TRIPLE TAKE

MR ENDED THOU
THUNDERDOME

BARTER GROUCH
TURBOCHARGER

EXPAND GLEE
APEX LEGEND

C	F	M	N	S	A	R	C	H	D	W	L	C	F	L	G	B	O	A	F	P
Y	D	H	E	R	I	F	T	I	P	S	F	I	G	Z	L	W	R	V	A	S
R	E	C	X	V	K	F	P	F	Z	D	K	L	F	R	K	E	F	P	W	
M	V	T	A	V	I	L	U	Z	K	S	Z	S	O	V	A	D	H	G	P	N
M	O	C	T	A	N	E	L	Q	R	M	A	S	T	I	F	F	Q	M	I	L
C	T	A	I	B	W	K	E	I	J	V	A	Y	M	A	I	L	A	B	X	M
T	I	P	V	T	Q	C	P	C	W	D	X	K	V	N	G	A	B	F	K	L
S	O	I	T	Q	S	P	M	C	L	S	Q	S	D	I	T	T	Y	E	D	P
R	N	T	L	Z	Z	U	V	T	K	I	C	E	I	X	W	L	D	R	O	E
U	W	Q	G	I	B	R	A	L	T	A	R	I	Q	Y	B	I	O	E	O	A
B	J	D	Y	G	L	M	V	C	A	D	L	V	H	Y	B	N	R	B	B	C
R	D	M	R	D	O	Z	N	D	H	K	T	R	I	P	L	E	T	A	K	E
E	B	O	N	X	O	A	P	B	N	H	H	A	E	B	I	J	Z	R	P	K
L	E	Z	B	E	D	X	C	O	N	Z	V	T	A	I	F	W	P	K	T	E
W	R	A	I	T	H	L	M	E	I	Q	D	N	Q	P	E	T	Z	P	A	E
O	I	M	I	H	O	E	G	H	W	B	A	N	G	A	L	O	R	E	M	P
R	W	B	H	J	U	R	M	E	H	D	H	O	P	G	I	Y	D	B	P	E
P	U	I	M	M	N	Q	F	L	V	O	Z	F	N	J	N	R	O	U	Y	R
P	P	Q	S	D	V	O	A	O	T	T	U	C	O	E	Y	L	G	N	Y	
N	E	U	W	F	C	N	H	U	T	K	V	W	N	Q	D	G	U	Q	I	T
R	R	E	J	H	G	O	Z	W	T	K	B	Q	L	P	E	A	K	I	O	
R	I	M	M	B	N	W	Y	U	I	N	P	U	W	T	T	L	D	R	L	D
H	A	V	O	C	H	A	O	G	A	I	T	P	R	J	F	J	R	W	I	M
P	B	W	O	N	W	C	Y	E	W	L	W	R	C	S	C	G	E	C	M	
R	R	I	Z	R	S	B	D	V	Z	Y	S	M	U	P	T	Y	J	B	W	J

6	5	3	2	9	7	8	4	1
8	4	2	1	3	5	6	7	9
9	7	1	6	8	4	5	2	3
4	1	9	5	2	8	3	6	7
5	2	8	3	7	6	9	1	4
3	6	7	4	1	9	2	5	8
2	3	6	8	4	1	7	9	5
7	8	4	9	5	2	1	3	6
1	9	5	7	6	3	4	8	2

5	4	8	7	9	1	6	3	2
3	7	6	5	2	8	9	1	4
9	2	1	6	3	4	8	5	7
4	1	9	8	5	3	2	7	6
6	8	5	4	7	2	3	9	1
2	3	7	1	6	9	5	4	8
8	5	3	2	1	7	4	6	9
1	6	4	9	8	5	7	2	3
7	9	2	3	4	6	1	8	5

1	4	8	5	2	6	7	9	3
2	3	7	1	8	9	4	6	5
6	5	9	4	7	3	1	8	2
8	6	5	3	1	7	9	2	4
7	1	4	2	9	5	6	3	8
9	2	3	6	4	8	5	7	1
3	7	2	9	5	4	8	1	6
4	8	1	7	6	2	3	5	9
5	9	6	8	3	1	2	4	7

8	4	1	9	7	2	6	5	3
3	7	9	4	6	5	1	2	8
5	2	6	8	3	1	9	7	4
9	8	5	6	2	4	3	1	7
1	3	4	7	5	9	2	8	6
7	6	2	3	1	8	5	4	9
2	9	7	1	4	6	8	3	5
6	5	3	2	8	7	4	9	1
4	1	8	5	9	3	7	6	2

PAGE 39

7	4	9	8	3	1	6	2	5
5	2	1	7	4	6	3	9	8
3	6	8	5	9	2	1	7	4
8	7	6	2	5	9	4	3	1
4	9	2	1	8	3	7	5	6
1	5	3	6	7	4	9	8	2
2	3	4	9	6	8	5	1	7
9	8	7	4	1	5	2	6	3
6	1	5	3	2	7	8	4	9

1	3	6	9	7	4	2	8	5
2	4	9	3	5	8	6	7	1
8	7	5	2	1	6	9	4	3
5	9	7	4	6	2	3	1	8
4	8	2	1	9	3	7	5	6
3	6	1	5	8	7	4	2	9
9	2	4	8	3	5	1	6	7
7	5	3	6	2	1	8	9	4
6	1	8	7	4	9	5	3	2

PAGE 55

PAGE 54

DIVE ONTO
DEVOTION

AD ACCESS
CASCADES

RIP DAFT HEN
PATHFINDER

HYDRA MOD
HYDRO DAM

BEAST SPLAT
BATTLE PASS

NU BOLD HOOD
BLOODHOUND

EYEBALL TAROT
BATTLE ROYALE

RAMJET SLUMP
JUMPMASTER

CLONKED KID SHOWN
KNOCKDOWN SHIELD

FIERCER KILL SLURPING
SKULLPIERCER RIFLING

PAGE 70

PAGE 71

77

SEE YOU IN THE CANYON SOON...